AF208437

THE GENIUS OF SIMPLICITY

LINDA WICKES

THE GENIUS OF SIMPLICITY

A SUZUKI METHOD® SYMPOSIUM

Summy-Birchard Inc.

© 1982 by Summy-Birchard Music
division of Summy-Birchard Inc.
Exclusive print rights administered by
Alfred Publishing Co., Inc.
ISBN 0-87487-261-8

CONTENTS

ABOUT SUZUKI is a series of publications dealing with the philosophy of early childhood education developed by Shinichi Suzuki. Beginning with the successful "mother tongue" approach to the teaching of violin and musicianship to very young children, his methodology has been expanded to include cello, viola, string ensemble, piano, and flute. The Suzuki emphasis on teaching the whole child in the way most natural to each child has gained worldwide acceptance. Suzuki teachers can be found in every corner of the globe, and educators have become increasingly interested in comparing the Suzuki approach to other pioneering trends in childhood education. "About Suzuki" publications make the exciting and thought-provoking concepts of this international forum equally accessible to educators, parents, students, and the general reader.

LINDA WICKES, author of "The Genius of Simplicity," is a graduate of Stephens College and the University of Oregon. As a violinist she is a member of the Eugene Symphony and the Oregon Bach Festival orchestra. As an educator she is an active member of the Suzuki Association of the Americas, American String Teachers' Association and the Oregon Music Teachers' Association, and she is a frequent university and institute lecturer. Ms. Wickes is also founder and director of Summer Strings Celebration, an annual workshop for string students of private teachers, ranging from three-year-old Suzuki students through advanced chamber music players.

INTRODUCTION

A COMBINATION of inspiration and irritation provoked me to write this book. The inspiration came from working with Suzuki method. As a teacher I felt the need for a positive, constructive approach, a method less arbitrary than I had been exposed to and yet with a solid structure, a well-built framework that would serve the student well. Once I "discovered" Suzuki method I felt a great sense of joy; at once challenged and yet comfortable, I sensed that I had finally "come home."

The irritation came from skeptics who imply that Suzuki method is a shallow and simplistic gimmick. This book is an answer, a rebuttal, to that implication.

There is a universality of musical and psychological concepts and techniques that, fitted together, make up Suzuki's method. Although some may consider it to be revolutionary, his method is based on ideas deeply rooted in the rich soil tilled by philosophers, educators, psychologists, and musicians, both performers and teachers. Great minds often run in the same paths, and some say there is nothing new under the sun. Suzuki, however, has correlated and integrated many seemingly ordinary, simple ideas into one creative and flexible method. The parts may not be new, but the synthesis is, and it is Suzuki's genius to have brought these elements together.

The reader of this book will, then, hear from Plato and Piaget, Ginott and Galamian, Havas and Holt and Heifetz, and many others. I quote them from their own writings or interviews in their areas of specialization, and have selected passages which show the relationship of their thoughts to those of Suzuki. Very few of the authors were addressing themselves specifically to Suzuki method, but each was expressing his independent thinking on matters which touch on or tie in to Suzuki's ideas.

Imagine yourself sitting in your own living room surrounded by this distinguished group. Enjoy the company.

1 THE PHILOSOPHY OF SUZUKI

E VERY child can be educated by the 'Mother Tongue' method. It was forty years ago when this astonishing fact occurred to me," says Shinichi Suzuki. "Children everywhere in the world were speaking in their own language; moreover, they did this fluently, which required a very high level of proficiency.

"From that very day I started to study . . . and observe the practicability of the 'Mother Tongue' method.

"As a result I learned that the natural method of teaching a child its mother tongue is a marvelous educational process. It fills the child with enthusiasm. . . .

"Sometime later I tried to adapt this method to music education for young children. I accepted a number of children without first auditioning them, and began to teach them violin experimentally, convinced that every child would develop. The children did show great progress and enjoyed the process" [38].

Maria Montessori had also observed the learning process both she and Suzuki named the "mother tongue" method. In *The Absorbent Mind* she wrote, "The child has a mind able to absorb knowledge. He has the power to teach himself. A single observation is enough to prove this. The child grows up speaking his parent's tongue, yet to grownups the learning of a language is a very great intellectual achievement. No one teaches the child, yet he comes to use nouns, verbs and adjectives to perfection" [27].

Pointing out, as does Suzuki, that the child learns the language he is exposed to, she noted that "An Indian baby taken to America, and placed in the care of Americans, learns to speak English and not Hindi. So his language does not come from the mother, but it is the child who takes in the language, just as he takes in the habits and customs of the people among whom he happens to be living. There is nothing hereditary, therefore, in any of these acquisitions. It is the child who absorbs material from the world about him. . . " [27].

Suzuki states firmly and frequently that good environmental conditions produce superior abilities, and that it is the environment at the earliest stages of infancy that is critical. "There is no use judging children's abilities from the training they receive five or six years *after* birth" [39].

"I have no doubt that people are born with hereditary physiological differences, but I believe that a person's abilities grow and develop depending on stimulation from the outside . . . I would say that a child can, at the very least, develop all his various abilities to the high level of his ability in using his mother tongue" [38].

"Not only in music, but in many other fields children are often educated in ways which stunt and damage their abilities. I believe that attention must be given to a child's education from the day of his birth" [26].

Although a strong spokesman for the effect of environmental influences on the child, Suzuki does recognize that "individuals . . . are born with inherently superior or inferior qualities, and differences in ability will no doubt occur because of these innate differences" [26].

Suzuki joins others in pleading the cause of parent education. "I wish the countries of the entire world could establish and carry out national policies for child training and care. . . . When you contemplate a carefully cultivated green field and think of the care taken in the raising and cultivation of it, you cannot help but wonder that all that went into that project should be denied to children; whereas if they, too, received the care that the field received, they would grow up to be good human beings with their respective abilities highly developed, who would build a good society.

"But the raising and educating of children must be

founded on a proper knowledge of how all this is to be accomplished. . . . I visited the Prime Minister and discussed with him the need for a national policy of child development. . . . The love that parents have for their children would be awakened to proper child development through the guidance of trained instructors and good character and ability would be promoted in every home" [38]. He spoke on this subject at the United Nations on the same occasion as cellist Pablo Casals.

Suzuki ardently believes that music has the power to improve the human spirit and open the heart, to make finer human beings of all those it touches. While this may seem overly sentimental to our modern, Western minds, he is in distinguished company. Plato said, "In order to become the right kind of a person, you must listen to the right kind of music" [18]. The concert violinist Fritz Kreisler said, "I always have felt that children should be brought into contact with fine music as early as possible because taste is molded when we are young. When we are older we are most comfortable in the surroundings we became accustomed to in early years. Since music builds character and fortifies against adversity in later life, it is most essential that young folks grow up with it through the years" [1].

"It may very well be music which will save the world," said Casals [26].

Yehudi Menuhin, another great concert violinist, describes his physical exercises to prepare the violinist for practice and continues, "To maintain himself in the best physical condition, the athlete knows the importance of exercise, sleep and proper diet. But I believe that the violinist, in addition, has a further obligation. He knows he cannot play and interpret unless his spiritual condition is as good as his physical. The state of mind, the state of nerve, the state of heart are as important as the state of muscle" [25].

And Beethoven's "Kyrie" in the Missa Solemnis bears the inscription "From the heart, may it go to the heart!"

Dr. Masaaki Honda, who has been associated with the movement Suzuki calls "Talent Education" for many years and who accompanies the Suzuki tour groups writes, in the Introduction to *Suzuki Concept*:

> ... our understanding of this phrase "Talent Education" applies not only to knowledge or technical skill but also to morality, building of character, and appreciating beauty. We know that these are human attributes acquired by education and environment. Thus our movement is not concerned with raising so-called prodigies, nor does it intend to emphasize just "early development." We must express it as a "total human education."
>
> I think it is clear now that the aim in Talent Education is not to make musicians. We should not set a road for the future of children. They should make their own choice of profession at a suitable age, and may choose music or another field [26].

To illustrate his emphasis on the whole child, Suzuki tells this story in his own book *Nurtured by Love:*

> The mother of one of my students came one day to inquire about her son. This student had good musical sense, practiced very well, and was a superior child. "Sensei [Professor], will my boy amount to something?" When the mother asked me like that, I answered laughingly, "No. He will not become 'something.' " It seems to be the tendency in modern times for parents to entertain thoughts of this kind. It is an undisguisedly cold and calculating educational attitude. If I hear things like this, I want to reply in a joking way. But the mother was alarmed and surprised by my answer. So I continued, "He will become a noble person through his violin playing. Isn't that good enough? You should stop wanting your child to become a professional, just a good money earner. This thought is concealed in

your question and is offensive. A person with a fine
and pure heart will find happiness. The only worry for
parents should be to bring up their children as noble
human beings. That is sufficient. If this is not their
greatest hope, in the end the child may take a road
contrary to their expectations. Your son plays the violin
very well. We must try to make him splendid in mind
and heart also" [39].

This point of view is sometimes deplored by those who
feel that all violin teaching should be geared toward a performing artist's needs. Yet very few students will indeed
become professionals, let alone concert artists.

Menuhin remarks amusingly, "I have met people who
have made a great success of their lives by knowing when to
give up the violin; but," he continues sympathetically, "it is
sad that so often they haven't even kept it up for their own
pleasure. And this is simply because they were badly
taught." And he goes on to talk of Suzuki and his ambition to
create a generation of amateurs. "The amateur—literally
one who loves—is the person who adores his work; and no
art, and no achievement in society, can flourish unless it is
based on thousands of people who are dedicated
amateurs—on people who love to paint, to build, to cook, to
play the violin" [25].

He believes that "Chamber music should be played . . . by
amateurs rather than by professionals. . . . It is my prayer and
hope that . . . when the present generation grow up, they
will have the means to play for themselves, for their friends,
for their families, to make chamber music at home" [25].

Public school music educators do not expect most of their
students to become professional musicians, and are un-
doubtedly grateful to turn out true amateurs.

An important tenet in Suzuki's philosophy is that learning
should be a pleasant experience. He asks for "Two minutes
five times a day, with joy." Rudolf Dreikurs, the psychiatrist,
writes, "Natural inclination is often stifled by : . . ambitious

parents insisting that children practice more.... They transform an art which should provide enjoyment and inspiration into a tortuous and tedious task. To be sure, nothing can be achieved without training; but training requires interest and stimulation . . . Parents should add stimulation but not pressure. Parents can play records, take him to concerts, help him appreciate music, admire his progress. . . . Conflict between parents and child prevent (sic) proper training . . . His inability is the result" [7].

Menuhin says, "even if he is a child, who can only practice ten minutes, it is important that these ten minutes be spent to the full value. . . . Practice must be looked upon as a joy and a privilege, not as a sentence. Too many young violinists with ambitious parents have been sentenced to work" [25].

Two renowned violin teachers speak of teaching much as Suzuki practices it. Ivan Galamian writes, "The teacher should be conscientious, patient, and even-tempered. Above all, he must have real love and enthusiasm for his work. Good teaching takes a measure of devotion that the teacher is unable to give unless his heart and soul are dedicated to it" [10].

And Kato Havas writes, "Teaching the violin, like going into the ministry, or nursing, is not merely a job, or profession, but a vocation. For, while a clergyman is responsible for the well-being of the soul, a nurse for the well-being of the body, a violin teacher should really be responsible for the free expression of both" [15].

2   START YOUNG

EDUCATORS are constantly becoming more aware of how much children learn in their earliest years. "The hottest area for research right now is not the earliest years, but the earliest *months* of life," writes Maya Pines in her book *Revolution in Learning*. "Psychologists increasingly believe that the roots of intellectual curiosity are laid during these months....

"The cognitive psychologists believe that the lives of all children could be made much richer if their abilities were developed systematically from the moment of birth" [29].

Describing his work with children, O. K. Moore writes, "Those who start younger do better . . . they have an easy, natural swing to their behavior—the older ones are more careful and deliberate. But a three-year-old will act as if he weren't paying attention." At that age he can tolerate a great many more errors in his own performance than even a six-year-old will accept. "By the time a child is three, he has achieved what is probably the most complex and difficult task of his lifetime—he has learned to speak" [29].

Montessori said, "The greatness of the human personality begins at the hour of birth." And she wrote, "Instead of leaving everything to chance, the child's growth at this time should be a matter for scientific care and attention" [27]. Many others concur. "Instead of ignoring the early years, it is our duty to cultivate them with the utmost care," wrote Alexis Carrel [5].

In his book on music aptitude Carl Seashore observed that "the physiological limit of pitch discrimination does not vary with age.... Eyes differ; even in childhood they may vary from the perfect to the near blind. Exactly so with hearing. There are differences in the quality of the psychophysic ear for pitch. So far as the ear is concerned, the child at five can probably hear as well as he ever will, and one important element in hearing is pitch. . . . A child can tell as well as an adult which of two tones is higher if he understands what is meant by higher . . . " [34].

Hearing specialists now know that the ear is fully capable of hearing all ranges of pitch at birth; in fact, after four months of gestation the hearing mechanism is complete [6]. The naming of pitch is what John Kendall calls a "social agreement" [20]. Therefore testing dependent on what a child can name and report on would not be possible until around three years of age, but he has been hearing pitch since birth.

Rosamund Shuter observed in *The Psychology of Musical Ability* that musicians have better pitch recognition on the first instrument to which they were regularly exposed than any other, even though subsequently they may take up a different instrument as their major one. She also notes that the ability to respond accurately to rhythmic patterns and keep a steady beat does not change substantially after the age of nine.

There is a significant correlation between the singing ability of young children and a musical environment, she writes. Some factors affecting their ability are mothers who sang to and with children, aid from other adults, family singing and playing, parents with musical background, and older brothers and sisters studying music. Home enrichment has a strong positive effect on younger children's interest in music. And, interestingly, children whose parents provide them with lessons are better adjusted emotionally than others [36].

Rudolf Dreikurs, the Adlerian psychiatrist, writes, "There are people who take no pleasure at all in music . . . they may be monotones—this is taken to indicate a complete lack of musical ability. But it has been proved that the assumed 'lack of a musical ear' is a protest against musical activity as a result of discouragement. . . . Children who have never been taught to sing at home may be stigmatized as unmusical when they sing at school. Thoughtless teachers [may] ridicule them . . . until their want of musical ability is taken as an established fact" [7].

Suzuki writes in this same vein, "Mothers often say to me, 'I am tone-deaf' in an effort to explain that their child is the same. They think it is hereditary and that there is nothing they can do about it. But just as nightingales are not born tone-deaf, neither are human infants. On the contrary, a baby absorbs perfectly any out-of-tune pitch of its mother's lullabies. It has a marvelous ear. That's why the child will later sing in the same way. Osaka children absorb the intricate Osaka dialect in exactly the same fashion.

"If a baby is brought up listening to a recording of a song out of tune, his ears will become accustomed to it, and it will be very hard for him to change later on. Thus, if we wanted to, we could make all children throughout the world tone-deaf" [39].

Willa Freeman Grunes, a clinical psychologist and mother of a Suzuki student, remarks that the Suzuki method makes use of a physiologically crucial period when the nervous system is still flexible. "Concentrated early experience with good music, including accurate intonation and rhythm, appears crucial to the development of 'natural' musical abilities. Mr. Suzuki is quite right, I think, that babies adapt to their musical environments in their cradles . . . ."

She also points out that starting music education at preschool age is socially and culturally compatible with the fact that the parents expect to spend time caring for and teaching their children, that the children are still learning their values from their parents, and that their self-picture is still in an initial formative stage, which can include being a musician. "The Suzuki student who starts early usually cannot later recall his first experiences with his instrument. It seems to him that he has always belonged with it; it has become part of his emergent self."

Not every young child who starts to study violin, however, will continue over the years, even though Suzuki ideally would like "no dropouts." For a very young student, quitting can feel like failure. Grunes says, "One of the dangers is that the Suzuki method can appeal to what I call the Pushy Parent." It can appeal to a person who is driven to fulfill his own ambitions vicariously through his child. A too-critical parent can push a child into a sense of failure at an age when it can become an integral part of the child's emerging self image. "When a pushy parent gets involved in his very young child's progress as compared with other children it can have a negative effect" [13].

If the parents can avoid ego-involvement in their child's progress, his violin study can be a pleasant mutual experience. For gifted children music training might be especially valuable. As a group they excel in reading, get higher grades, participate in more extracurricular activities and have more hobbies and interests than their less gifted counterparts. In Research on the Talented Miriam Goldberg writes, "The amount that a gifted child will learn is far more related to the amount of knowledge to which he is exposed than to any other single factor" [12]. For any child exposure is a basic requirement for learning: children who have never heard French spoken will not speak it; deaf children have great difficulty learning to speak any language at all.

Suzuki describes the happy movements and smiles of recognition a six-month-old baby will give when he hears the music he has heard repeatedly. Describing how a certain piece of music can become like a "security blanket" for a child, Marjorie McDonald tells of a two-year-old who ordered her father to "Play Bach!" when she was put to bed [24]. In our house it is, "Put on the Mozart!"

3 STEP-BY-STEP MASTERY

THE two points Suzuki says are essential to his method are the training of the ear at a very early age and the step-by-step mastery of each element of violin playing. By arranging the musical materials in careful progression, Suzuki has built into the literature the foundations for the ability to succeed in each successive piece of music. It is important that each step be thoroughly mastered before the next one is taken. Used by a conscientious teacher and a parent who understands the importance of this principle, the method is a successful program of instruction.

The student does not follow a timetable other than that of his own mastery of the material. A three-year-old might take a year to learn the set of variations on "Twinkle, Twinkle, Little Star" which are the first works in the method, yet an older child could learn a new piece in a few weeks. It is axiomatic that the beginning stages are much slower than later stages. Suzuki, along with Plato, believes "The beginning is the most important part of the work" [31].

In *Human Performance* the psychologists Fitts and Posner explain the way people learn a new skill:

> During the early phase of skill learning it is usually necessary to attend to cues, events, and responses that later go unnoticed. In learning a dance step, one attends to kinesthetic and visual information about the feet, information which is later ignored. Some instructors report that one of the most difficult things for many beginners to learn is to process information concerning their own limbs . . . .
>
> The early or cognitive stage of learning, when instructions and demonstrations are the most effective . . . allows for the selection of an initial repertoire of subroutines . . .

... during the intermediate phase of skill learning, old habits which have been learned as individual units during the early phase of skill learning, are tried out and new patterns begin to emerge.

During the final phase of skill learning, component processes become increasingly autonomous, less directly subject to cognitive control, and less subject to interference from other ongoing activities or environmental distractions. In this phase, skills require less processing. This means that they can be carried on while new learning is in progress ... Thus a well-practiced task like walking may not interfere with talking [9].

Sometimes as a game Suzuki will ask children to tell what they ate for lunch or say their names and addresses while they are playing the violin, to demonstrate that they have arrived at this final phase where the skill has become so automatic that they can carry on the mechanics of playing while doing something else, finally so free of the technical problems of playing as to think only of the art. "Art begins where technique ends," wrote the great violinist and teacher Leopold Auer [2].

The teacher, using the framework of the method, breaks down the skills to be learned into small components and matches each one to the learning ability of the student. A range of activities in teaching any concept is valuable. Learning should begin with physical activities, with muscular movement preceding verbal descriptions. Every step in forming a concept should be worked through. Detailed descriptions of a child's cognitive and intellectual development can be studied in the writings of child psychologist Jean Piaget.

What J. M. Hunt calls the "problem of the match" is essential [29]. The right balance must exist between what the child feels confident of and the challenge of new steps to be taken, new problems to solve. The teacher matches the work to the child's ability to cope with it. Jerome Bruner points out that "corrective information that exceeds the information-processing capacities of a learner is obviously wasteful" [4]. Or put another way, "An effective teacher is one who finds out what a child already knows so that she may do a better job of helping him learn more" [35].

"Mistakes are not to be merely criticized as mistakes," says Menuhin. "Any fool can hear a scratch or an uneven, out-of-tune note on the violin. That is hardly worth mentioning. What is obvious, and obvious to the student too, does not have to be stressed. It is what the student cannot explain and cannot correct that is the teacher's responsibility" [25].

In *Principles of Training* Holding supports the training of skills in small steps with positive feedback. "It does seem desirable on commonsense grounds to make knowledge of progress as favourable as possible, an effect which can be arranged by manipulating the target set for the learner. One way of keeping failure to the minimum is to set him to better his own previous performance, rather than to reach an arbitrary standard. As the size or complexity of a task increases it becomes inefficient for the beginner to tackle the whole task. Discrete, repetitive or serial tasks are easily subdivided into parts which may then be practised separately. . . . the best solution seems to be a form of gradual progression in which simple skills are slowly transformed into more demanding activities. The units in early practice of this kind are therefore *small wholes* rather than *parts*.

"At every stage of programmed learning the trainee is asked to do only what is within his grasp. He is *prompted* throughout and *corrected* where necessary, but has chosen the response himself on the basis of the information available to him. The right amount of information is available, because the programmer knows what he is trying to achieve and has experimented with ways of achieving it" [16].

Although Holding is not writing about teaching an instrument exclusively, but any kind of skill training from flying an airplane to running a race, the principles are constant. The execution of the "training program" lies in the hands of the trainer or teacher, however, and the success of the program depends on the teacher's skill in matching the challenges and successes to the learning ability of the trainee or student.

The cellist Orlando Cole says, "Since so-called 'natural talents' are extremely rare, it is the student of average or little talent who most needs the help of better teaching methods and also a very clear analysis of his problems" [1].

Suzuki says that advancing a child on a preordained track at a specified rate of speed produces frustration on the part of child and teacher alike. Allowing, even encouraging, a child to take as long as he needs to master concepts and skills requires parents and teachers to adapt themselves to the rhythm of the child.

One small step toward a skill, well done and well appreciated, is more meaningful than promises of concertos and concertmasterships in the dim future.

"If we start the pupil climbing an interminable range of arid hills, encourage him with tales of vast views and flowing streams far ahead and refuse on principle to give him so much as a drink of water, he is exceedingly apt to leave his bones by the trail" [36].

4 LEARNING BY LISTENING

YOUNG children are natural mimics; Suzuki method takes advantage of their desire and ability to imitate. Suzuki asks that the child be exposed to music from birth, and that a limited number of compositions be played repeatedly so he recognizes them. Before violin lessons begin, the child will have started listening to the recording of the music he will eventually learn. Having recorded examples as teaching aids is not a new idea, but with Suzuki method a complete and logical sequence of the material beginning with the very first steps is available.

Psychologist Steven Keele writes that one component of skill learning is an accurate template of desired feedback. ". . . sometimes the template may be established prior to learning movements. This may be the procedure underlying the outstanding success of the Suzuki method of violin teaching. In the Suzuki method very young children are exposed to selected pieces of music, sometimes for months or years, prior to actually handling an instrument. Perhaps the detailed music templates that the children store in memory allow them to subsequently recognize errors in their own sound production and alter the sequencing of movements that lead to the sound" [19].

The process of rote teaching is easier if the student already has a clear mental image of the music to be learned. One could say that the child already knows the music and that the teacher only needs to teach the mechanics of how to play it. The recording also provides a model for the sound of a violin; just as a child needs a model of precise sounds for learning his own language, so he needs a model for the tone of a violin. "Sensitiveness to tone should be established early, and no amount of listening to poor tone, whether self-produced, or otherwise, will create a desirable tonal image" [21].

Rosamund Shuter suggests that "The development from babbling all possible sounds to speaking one's native language is probably paralleled in music by the development from the earliest vocalizations to singing the notes of a specific musical scale" [36].

In "The Suzuki System: A Critical Evaluation" Kenneth Sarch points out that "the principle of 'imitation' in language learning is a simple observation compared with the vast studies and theories dealing with language acquisition, child education, linguistics, and the studies of the mind" [32]. Language acquisition is indeed complex. Imitation plays only a part in a child's language learning, but it does undeniably exist as an essential part of the process. ". . . language . . . is necessarily acquired in a context of imitation," writes Piaget. [28].

The authors of a study on "Imitation in Language Development" note that children imitated words they did not yet know, but they did not imitate words they used spontaneously. There is a clear trend for individual words that were originally imitative to become predominantly spontaneous at later times. A child "did not imitate what he knew best and he did not imitate what he knew nothing about . . . he imitated utterances in just those categories which were to become fully productive at a subsequent time but which were currently beyond his productive capacity" [3].

Similarly, students are attentive to the recordings and the teacher's demonstrations of a new piece, the one they are starting to learn or want to learn, but show little if any interest in listening to or watching very elementary work which they have already understood and feel they have completed.

Even though linguists still puzzle over the innate understanding of syntax each child seems to be born with, there is no denying the simple fact that each child learns to speak the language he hears.

The teacher demonstrates, the child copies. ". . . demonstrations . . . show the learner what he is required to do, thus setting a standard against which he can compare his own efforts. They also provide a basis for imitation," writes Dennis Holding in *Principles of Training*. Verbal instructions are less helpful than demonstrations. "Translating words into actions is a further process, itself requiring attention. . . . It is possible to disrupt the [student's] performance in quite a lasting way by the over-elaboration of instructions" [16]. Experiments in training show that breaking up the instructions and spacing them out through the learning of the task amounts to verbal guidance which is extremely efficient. Verbal and motor activities are, however, separate; what is learned verbally cannot always be translated into action, nor can learned actions always be put into words. Havas puts it thus, "No one can learn even to ride a bicycle from a set of written instructions. . ." [15].

Describing learning by imitation, Piaget writes, "In a behavior pattern of sensori-motor imitation the child begins by imitating in the presence of the model (for example, a movement of the hand), after which he may continue in the absence of the model. . ." [28].

Simplifying the learning situation by eliminating as many distractions as possible helps to focus the child's attention on the violin itself, the sound being produced, and the process of producing it; he concentrates on listening and playing.

Rote learning implies playing from memory. An extra benefit of the long period of playing from memory is an added ease in memorizing; in fact the process becomes automatic since all learning in the early stages is from memory, and this helps remove some of the fear and stage-fright in later performances. Menuhin notes that "memory feeds memory" and that the Western violinist "is usually taught from the printed page and this accounts for much of the dullness of Western violin teaching" [25].

The violinist Joseph Szigeti says, "The aid of memory is of

great importance. The best work, even technically, can be done only when the printed music has been done away with" [1].

Suzuki-trained children display impressive confidence in performance, appearing to be relaxed and enjoying themselves, perhaps because their long training from memory makes them trust themselves. In his book *How Children Learn* John Holt says, "The children who always forget things in school may not forget so much because their memories are bad, as because they never dare trust their memories. Even when they are right, they still feel wrong" [17].

Rote teaching continues side by side with reading music when the child is older, because of its advantages for teaching technique and memorization.

When a child should learn to read music depends on several factors: the age of the child and how long he has been playing; his facility and degree of competence with his instrument, including maintaining good positions, pitch and tone; the child's ability to read symbols; his need because of the complexity of the music he is learning or the fact that he is playing in ensembles; his interest and desire. The average three-year-old would neither be physically nor mentally ready to learn to read music. Nor could he learn the complex technical skills required to play the violin and simultaneously focus his attention on the complex codes representing musical sounds. An older beginner might spend a shorter period of time rote learning.

"Certainly, the ability to read music is necessary for continued musical development," writes John Kendall, "and rote playing, plus memorization, should never be a substitute for it" [21].

There is nothing inherent in Suzuki method that makes music reading more difficult to learn. The very fact that it is delayed may whet the child's appetite.

Reading experts agree that "there is no single best way of learning to read, and therefore no single best way of teaching children to read. Wise reading teachers make appropriate use of all the tools and techniques available at the time most suitable for using them. They do not speak of *the* method of teaching reading because they understand that teaching reading is a composite procedure that assembles and uses the best methods that professional theory, research, and the practical common sense of competent teachers have been able to devise" [22].

Kendall writes, "It is logical to expect that in teaching music reading skills, a technical preparation on an instrument, as a means of expressing the musical symbols, will *improve* the possibilities of success for any of the methods currently used by music teachers. *Speaking* a language precedes reading skills, and we emphasize reading readiness as a factor. The same sequence is implied in music, if the variable of reading readiness is handled in a way similar to the language teaching methods. Specifically, the fact that a child already knows *how* to play what the symbols indicate should be a distinct advantage in teaching reading" [21].

In America our children are often able to join school music programs, ensembles and orchestras, but these are relatively scarce in Japan. Thus an American child might need and want to learn to read music sooner than his Japanese counterpart. However, the period of rote teaching develops listening skills and provides ear training which cannot be matched in a school orchestra with many instruments playing different parts, pitches and rhythms.

The eventual goal of the teacher, as of the parent, is to develop the child's own ability to help himself, to evaluate and to develop his own judgment and individuality. In *Principles of Training,* Holding writes, "If the action is an end in itself, as in ballet, the learner is forced to rely upon his perception of sameness and differences in his own and the instructor's performance. Very often the instructor will supply verbal knowledge of results, but gradually the learner must refine his own standards of judgment" [16].

Galamian writes that "a teacher should try to encourage a personal initiative while at the same time constantly striving to better the student's understanding and to improve his taste and sense of style. The teacher must always bear in mind that the highest goal should be for him to make the student self-sufficient" [10]. "The goal of training," writes Dreikurs, "is to render itself superfluous" [7]. Galamian adds a word of warning: "To build self-confidence too soon can be almost as dangerous as not to build it at all" [10].

Havas and Galamian both write of the importance of listening and developing the ability to listen. Havas points out that the way the hand or arm is held is not the ultimate goal but the result is "judged *by the degree of excellence in tone production*" [15]. Galamian concurs: The *sound* produced has to be under permanent scrutiny. The ear is always the final judge in deciding what is good and what is not" [10]. Joseph Szigeti said ". . . the real art is for the pupil to acquire the uncanny ability to listen to his own work" [1].

Havas says the ability to listen continuously and carefully is one of the greatest deficiencies in young violinists. And she writes, "Instead of spending hours trying to train the fingers to play in tune, we should train our minds to hear the tune" [15].

5 GROUP LESSONS AND PERFORMANCES

U NISON playing in groups is a regular and important part of Suzuki method. The children have a common repertoire, and the group performances give them opportunities to play for fun and experience but without the strain and competitiveness of orchestral work. Younger children see and hear older, more advanced students, and advanced students gain ease and familiarity with actual performance, no matter how small their audience may be.

Suzuki says, "Parents who do not understand children think they are paying for the private lessons and that the group lessons are just recreation periods. So although they make sure that their children attend the private lessons, they often fail to bring them to the group lessons. But the fact is that what the children enjoy most is the group playing. They play with children who are more advanced than they are; the influence is enormous, and is marvelous for their training. This is the real talent education" [39].

Instruction and criticism can be more palatable and easier to take in a group where no one person is singled out. John Wooden, the great basketball coach, used a technique described as "scold/reinstructions" in training sessions. "These scold/reinstructions are often shouted during a group activity when no one can be sure who is the offending member, and consequently everyone tries to put himself in order" [40].

Violinist Milstein's teacher, when he was seven years old, "stressed group work very firmly. We were with him twice a week, and eight or ten pupils would come to the lessons. We learned from each other" [1].

Grunes expresses some concern about the group exposure. "Because the method involves group work and because the accomplishment is visible the strong motivational influences can easily become a visible, measurable failure if a child has not progressed at the same rate of speed as his peers. Parents, too because of their involvement in the method, may feel a sense of failure if their child is not progressing as well as another, and may even blame their children for making them look like inferior parents. A parent who feels very competitive may try to push the child too hard and interfere with the child's enjoyment of his work" [13].

Teachers may feel the same sense of competition, especially at the large institutes, knowing their students' progress can be measured and compared with others'.

Ambitious parents and teachers are not confined to the ranks of Suzuki method, however, and Suzuki urges that each child's progress be recognized, appreciated and measured only against himself.

The widespread publicity given to the large group performances may, unfortunately, promote the misconception that Suzuki method is a group teaching program.

Critic Sarch objects to "the classroom idea of applying the same standards of progress for all regardless of ability." He writes, "Stress on group achievement, although itself a stimulation for the young, results, in the long run, in the acceptance of an average standard in place of the encouragement of the full potential of the individual. In other words, some play right, some do not, but the average effect covers up the inaccuracies. The favoring of group discipline (keeping together) and consistency (repeating the piece always the same way) becomes stifling for future growth and development" [32].

Group playing in unison is not unlike being in the first-violin section of an orchestra, where the discipline of keeping together is looked upon quite favorably. In a Suzuki-style group lesson or performance, the teacher serves as leader and the children follow. Sometimes a child will be chosen to be leader for a piece and the group must follow that leader's tempo and style.

"The concert master, the leader, the first violinist in an orchestra, holds a unique position in the violinist's world," writes Menuhin. "He must submit to the discipline of the group and maintain the inspiration and freedom of a soloist. While playing in unison with his group he cannot allow himself to do anything erratic. He must play as planned, with the same bowings and fingerings and inflections" [25].

Group playing provides practice in performing accurately bowings, attacks, entrances, dynamics and style. In addition to unison playing, group lessons may include a variety of skill-reinforcing games and exercises. Students often take this opportunity to play a work in progress or to try out a finished performance in a setting free of the tension of a recital or audition. These frequent informal performances help develop confidence and poise; the student who has played with others and in front of others from the very beginning is more likely to feel secure than one who is asked to perform alone in a recital a few times a year.

It is not the aim of group work to make every violinist like every other. Assisting a student to find his own individuality is an important part of a teacher's responsibility. Perhaps those who fear that group work levels out individual talents and makes the children all alike are underestimating the innate strength of children and the careful individual attention each Suzuki student receives in his private lessons.

6 PEDAGOGY AND TECHNIQUE

S UZUKI violin technique is based on a solid foundation of bow control and necessary left hand skills. He starts by making steps toward control as simple as possible so that the young child will have the maximum chance of success. For example, the bow is much easier to handle in the middle or upper-middle part using short strokes. Long, even, whole bows require great control, so Suzuki postpones whole bows and starts with short, firm strokes. The length of the bow to be used is usually marked with tapes on the bow. Similarly, the fingerboard is marked with tapes so that the child can find the right place to set down each finger; thus he is hearing his own playing in tune and thereby training his own ear as he plays.

Galamian also starts from the square of the arm. "The control of the bow is easiest and most natural near the square position, and it is best, therefore, to begin the study of the bow stroke at the square and to work from there toward the point and the frog" [10]. John Kendall writes, "A basic tenet of learning is progression from the simple to the complex. Yet how slow we have been in string teaching to depart from the difficult whole bow legato, as a first step. . . . Beginning instead with short, rapid strokes near the middle of the bow, in repeated patterns which can be interrupted, seems a much more sensible procedure" [21].

Suzuki teaches violin playing, like Fred Polnauer, for example, as a "motion-gestalt in which the whole and parts determine each other mutually and where the whole retains the primacy" [30]. Bernard Fischer describes it thus: "Gestalt exponents claim that the violin and bow are extensions of the body. For instance, Suzuki emphasizes the importance of the larger muscles in bow-arm activity in fast playing as well as in slow playing. Wrist and finger movement of the bow-arm very rarely act independently, but almost always follow the action of the arm, shoulder, and at times the body. The whole is of prime importance and the parts determine each other, whether it is the bow-arm or the left arm" [8].

Milstein says tennis is like bowing. "One must swing from the shoulder—it is not so much strength that is required as swing" [1]. Suzuki amuses his students by pretending to throw a baseball to demonstrate the swing and "follow-through" in bowing.

"You should have the feeling that the bow is a continuation of your arm, and part of the wrist. Just as the violin, on the other hand, is a continuation of the other arm," says Jascha Heifetz [1]. The cellist Orlando Cole said, "I consider the physical basis of string playing as being akin to any branch of athletics. . . . string teaching should be as specific and meticulous as good athletic coaching!" [1].

Havas writes, "It is impossible to overestimate the importance of a natural, and as a result, correct way of holding the violin. The whole future development of the player may depend on whether the violin becomes an obstacle, or an extension of the body" [15]. And later in her book, "it is not enough to say 'relax,' or 'loosen up.' Such a direction becomes of real value only when every step towards achieving relaxation and looseness has been so clearly explained and experienced that it would seem ridiculous to do anything else. That is why it is so important to deal separately with each part of the body that is involved in playing . . ." [15].

". . . the highest degree of motility of the whole body is a prerequisite for . . . technique," writes Polnauer, and asks for a "minimum of tension both in static and dynamic muscle activity" [30].

In 1908 Edith Winn wrote in *The Child Violinist,* "Beauty of tone is not compatible with awkwardness of body. I have stressed body gymnastics," which she describes in detail, to develop good posture, relaxation, and strength [42].

Menuhin devotes a great deal of time and thought to the physical preparation for violin practice and has given directions for many exercises for the whole body. He explained to a student, "Each time you use a muscle unnecessarily—each time you use more than the one you need and don't let the others rest, you're building up residual tension whereby the muscles get used to remaining in a state of high tension to no purpose . . . [and] you will never be able to get a pure, clean, correct motion" [25].

Some of Suzuki's games are meant to help the students develop the ability to move and respond quickly, and to hold the violin and bow easily and naturally. Sometimes he has them walk around while playing, or talk, or laugh at his clowning, to prevent any build-up of physical or psychological tension.

Suzuki's bow hold produces maximum tone power along with flexibility and control. Many great violinists use very similar bow holds, though of course no two hands are exactly alike. For an excellent example, photographs of Shmual Ashkenasi's bow grip and close-ups of many others in *The Way They Play* should be seen [1].

The Suzuki repertory is arranged so that the first pieces are played in the same key and with the same finger pattern. His theory is that staying in one key for a long time helps to develop the sensitivity to correct pitch better than moving around through many keys very early. The simple finger pattern establishes a strong left hand shape. The first pieces are on the A and E strings only, not only because they sound better on the small violins, but because the bow arm position is easier.

The study material is drawn from the music being learned. The young child finds it easier and more enjoyable to play a tune with which he is already familiar rather than a mechanical drill. Ottakar Sevcik, violinist and teacher, wrote systematically and progressively graded exercises for the violin. Yet, no matter how scientifically thorough Sevcik's technical exercises may be, they are certainly not fun. Suzuki believes that everything that needs to be learned can be found in the music itself.

Asked by Applebaum about the use of etudes, violinist Alexander Schneider replied, "I do regret that much time is spent on so many of the etudes which have very little if any value musically. The fascinating point is that there is so much material which is at once wonderful music and which have (sic) the same technical value." He added, "I would go so far as to say we can match every Kreutzer study with a Bach movement" [1].

Szigeti concurs, "advanced pupils need utilize very little of the general studies...the literature is so rich with interesting, very valuable passages—it has all that one could possibly require of almost any phase of violin playing....A good deal depends upon the inventiveness of the pupil. He must be able to diagnose his failings..." [1].

The teacher, of course, must be prepared to help the student analyze and recognize his weaknesses and guide him in creative ways to approach the music and the technical problems therein. Critics who say that Suzuki method is an easy way out may not have fully understood the tasks involved in guiding a student through the problems to be solved in each phrase of each composition.

In language, expatiation—the use of words or concepts in different contexts and under different circumstances—makes learning deeper and more lasting. So in music, there can be many different elements emphasized. The creative teacher may ask for concentration on specific areas of need, much as a doctor prescribes for different illnesses. He will also find it is easier to introduce new technical matters such as shifting, vibrato, or new bowings in simple, familiar material, so that the student need concentrate on only one new point at a time.

Suzuki uses a limited repertory and demands constant growth in the excellence of performance of familiar pieces.

"The natural tendency of teachers, students, and parents is to measure progress in terms of the amount of material covered," writes Kendall. "This tendency needs re-examining, especially in connection with developing technique and security of tone production. Could we not encourage the idea that a student who can produce the best tone, or show the most bowing facility, or play the best in tune, is the real achiever?" [21].

7 PARENTS AND PRACTICING AND PSYCHOLOGY

KNOWING how much a child learns even in infancy, we can see how crucial the parents and the environment created by them are to the child's learning. When a child of three or four starts to study an instrument as difficult as the violin, one does not expect him to direct his practice by himself. Suzuki acknowledges the parents as full partners in the child's musical training. He prefers to have a parent take violin lessons first, using the small instrument which will eventually belong to his child. The child comes along to the lessons and also attends lessons, groups, and performances of other students, until he becomes eager to try the violin himself. Meanwhile the parent has learned the rudiments of technique, enough to guide the young student.

Usually the child, being more flexible than his parent, surpasses him rather quickly, and the teacher and parent move in a different direction, with parent attending lessons and taking notes, trying out bowholds and fingerings, but not necessarily playing the violin. William Starr notes, too, that if the child is over three his desire to imitate his parents may not be as strong as his desire to be independent [37].

Speaking of his own childhood, Nathan Milstein said, "I started to play the violin not because I was drawn to it, but because my mother forced me to. She insisted upon regular daily practice. For every child, no matter how well endowed by nature, has to be wisely guided at the start. Oh yes, I was attracted to music. I wanted to hear it and I wanted to make it. But I had to be forced to learn how to make it. My mother sensed my affinity for music and made me practice regularly. Only when I progressed far enough to feel the music itself in my playing did I practice willingly and eagerly" [1].

Mothers can not only see to it that their children practice regularly, but they can also guide and shape the quality of the practicing. Leopold Auer, the great teacher, wrote, "I tell my pupils that . . . when they practice without observing and criticizing themselves they merely develop and perfect their faults. They are worse than wasting their time" [2].

Galamian also stresses the quality of practice. "One of the most important things that a teacher ought to teach his students is, therefore, the technique of good practice. He has to impress on his students that practice has to be a continuation of the lesson, that it is nothing but a process of self-instruction in which, in the absence of the teacher, the student has to act as the teacher's deputy, assigning himself definite tasks and supervising his own work. . . . Practice . . . lacking direction and control is a waste of time and effort. Not only does it not achieve what it sets out to do, but also it can sometimes be positively harmful. Mistakes are repeated over and over again, and the ear becomes impervious to faulty sounds. . . . It is important, of course, that the practice time is utilized well throughout, and that practicing becomes a daily habit" [10].

Menuhin writes, "an earnest and serious approach is important. . . . Obviously it is important for the teacher and the parent to instill the proper attitude of discipline and seriousness. . . . Once the child has chosen the violin and has lessons, his training must be respected . . ." [25].

Samuel Applebaum asked Galamian, "What about practicing during one's early years?"

"If we analyze the development of the well-known artists," he replied, "we see that in almost every case the success of their entire career was dependent upon the quality of their practicing. In practically each case, the practicing was constantly supervised either by the teacher or an assistant to the teacher. The lesson is not all. Children do not know how to work alone. The teacher must constantly teach the child how to practice" [1].

Before the child has developed the ability to organize and analyze his own practicing, the parent serves as assistant to the teacher, supervising, giving direction and purpose to each practice session, and offering encouragement and moral support throughout. This requires skill, tact, perserverance, and a host of imaginative approaches. The parents' role, especially when the children are young beginners, can be the backbone, or the crux—the point upon which the whole succeeds or fails.

Not only must the parent become a trained assistant so that his advice to the student will be technically and musically correct, but his guidance must also be emotionally and psychologically satisfying. Many parents find being a "Suzuki parent" the most difficult and challenging job they have ever tackled. And many find they learn how to improve all their relationships with their children, for the psychological principles and techniques inherent in Suzuki's approach carry over into other areas of family life.

Dreikurs, for example, writes, "Teachers could learn a great deal of practical psychology from salespeople who are not permitted to blame the customer if he shows sales resistance" [7]. And Sheehy writes, "Let us work harder on producing good material and less on pushing children around" [35]. Suzuki operates on these principles, making the work appealing, and selling the children on it and on the joys of playing the violin. Again Sheehy says, "Can you recall the glow that you experienced when someone approved something you had been doing and how you made every effort to do it better? Living with children in such a way offers the kind of soil for learning that cannot possibly be achieved with artificial motivation" [35]. Ideally, music is its own reward. Suzuki does not use charts, pins or prizes; the triumph is in being able to play a piece well and going on to the next one. Suzuki does, however, listen to thousands of tapes of a few special "graduation" pieces and sends back a diploma and his comments.

We have already noted how Suzuki method makes constructive use of peer-group pressure, with a circle of friends who also play the violin giving support. Modeling is a part of the picture, where a child who plays well provides a model for the other children to imitate. A teacher or parent can also serve as the model. "The example of greatest artistry is Wooden's use of modeling. His demonstrations are rarely longer than five seconds, but they are of such clarity as to leave an image in memory much like a textbook sketch" [40].

We have also seen that the parent becomes an active partner with the child and teacher, instead of a disciplinarian who enforces but does not participate in practice time. The parent also must practice for his role, and the teacher may need to help the parent learn how he may best help his child. The parent needs to understand the teacher's instructions, the correct procedures for accomplishing a given task, and the best ways of encouraging his child.

Grunes directs our attention to the "patterns of reinforcement inherent in the method (the concern of behavioristic psychologists)," and says, "we can see from another point of view why the method is so effective. Good Suzuki parents and teachers are trained to use praise as positive reinforcement very frequently, and to avoid criticism as much as possible. Gentle guidance and demonstration are to take the place of most critical comments. Repetition and shaping over a long period of time ensure ever increasing mastery at higher and higher levels" [13]. Shaping may be explained as taking the "behaviors . . . in his repertoire and reinforcing those that are similar to the goal behavior, gradually requiring that [they] be more and more similar to the goal behavior to be reinforced" [23].

Grunes uses a Suzuki teacher to demonstrate how she works with parents: "It is my hope that the budding speech therapists I teach will be inspired by her methods of ensuring parent involvement, of using the parent to teach their own children on the days between formal lessons, and of influencing the parent to use the supportive techniques which the teacher demonstrates—the frequent praise, the lack of negative criticism, the sense of fun and play, etc. Not only speech therapists, but many clinical psychologists, pediatricians, social workers, educators, etc., could benefit from what Suzuki teaches his teachers along these lines" [13].

Suzuki teaches his teachers and parents to notice and praise one thing the child has done right, even if it is minute in comparison to all the things he may have done wrong—even if it is only that he tried to play when the teacher asked him to. Then at least the child will be willing to try again. He says, "Good. Now try again. See if you can do it this way."

Havas comments on the importance of what the behaviorists call "contingent" approval. "By encouragement however I do not mean 'false praise.' Because nobody realizes the insincerity of false praise more quickly than the player himself. By encouragement I mean an atmosphere of trust during lessons, a feeling of working toward something positive; of absolute confidence on the part of the pupil, not so much in the teacher, as in the possibility of his own progress" [15].

Because the steps are small enough and well enough organized that a sense of progress is almost always felt, especially in the early books "... one can hardly imagine a closer approximation to a cognitive structure which is ideal for developing strong positive motivation in the child—as well as in his parent—for the attainment of well defined goals. It is an educator's dream," says Grunes [13].

Teaching is akin to strategic therapy. The therapist must "identify solvable problems, set goals, design interventions to achieve those goals, examine the responses..." The therapist (or teacher) "attempts to gain a small response and then build upon it, amplifying that response until he has achieved the goal..." [14].

Step-by-step learning is also akin to programmed learning. Writing about this, Holding says, "instructional programmes are intended to permit individual learners to make responses at their own rates. A high proportion of the student's responses are right, because the forms of words which constitute the programme items or steps are designed to *prompt* the correct answers. The steps which make up the programme are arranged in an orderly sequence, and are preferably of a size and kind determined by preliminary trials to lead the learner efficiently from the known to the unknown. Up to a point the smaller the size of step the better." He notes that prompting for correct response is more effective than allowing many errors: "The fact that efficient performance depends upon knowledge of results does not imply that all learning must take place by trial and error. The methods of physical, visual and verbal guidance are all directed towards limiting the learning of errors . . ." He recommends "letting the learner know where he stands by assessing his *progress*," arranging a "break when the learner shows signs of fatigue," spacing practice periods to allow time for mental practice and practicing the parts of a task separately. "Most tasks worth learning need to be subdivided. . . . Where tasks are only awkwardly divisible into parts, as in high-diving, it seems reasonable to attain them by *gradual progression*," making the dive a bit higher each time [16].

Studies in *Research in Music Behavior* confirm that undirected practice is far less effective than model-supported practice and planned and directed practice [43]. Although filling out charts for time practiced resulted in significantly more time spent practicing, there was no discernible difference between performance improvement in the group using charts and the group that was not [41].

Further studies show that classes receiving high percentages of approval from their teachers were more attentive and more orderly than those where negative attitudes, criticism, and disapproval were more prevalent.

Praise and approval must be appropriate, accurate, specific, and honest to be effective. More information is conveyed by descriptive praise, such as commending one crucial note played with good intonation, and a greater sense of accomplishment is felt by the student, than from evaluative statements about the person, such as "What a good little girl you've been—you went to your room and practiced a whole half hour!" The child feels his efforts are recognized by specific praise; he knows how hard he has worked to accomplish that one detail.

In his book, *Between Parent and Teenager,* Dr. Haim Ginott says, just as Havas did, "Praise is not flattery. Flattery is insincere and expedient. Praise is a sincere, positive evaluation of a person or an act. Yet certain kinds of sincere praise may bring results opposite to those expected . . .[because] praise is an evaluation. And evaluation is uncomfortable. The evaluator sits in judgement, and the judged are anxious. . . . Praise that evaluates personality or character is unpleasant, and unsafe. . . . Praise that describes efforts, accomplishments, and feelings is helpful and safe" [11].

Ginott also warns against combining praise and criticism, described as a "psychological sandwich: two pieces of praise with blame in between." Ginott says, "It is best not to mix criticism with praise. It is easier and less confusing to cope with honest praise, or honest criticism, than with a dishonest mixture of them" [11].

He urges "descriptive recognition. . . . Our words should describe clearly what we like and appreciate about his work, efforts, achievement, consideration, or creation. We describe the specific event and our specific feelings. [The child] draws general conclusions about his personality and character. When our statements are realistic and sympathetic, his inferences are positive and constructive" [11]. This is much like Havas' speaking of an atmosphere of trust, of working toward something positive, and the pupil having confidence in the possibility of his own progress.

Ginott prescribes a similarly factual and non-evaluative

approach to criticism. "Constructive criticism has one main function: to point out what has to be done in the situation. Helpful criticism does not address itself to the personality. It deals with the difficult event. It never attacks the person; it talks to his condition." Just as Menuhin notes the futility of pointing out the obvious, Ginott writes, "Most criticism is unnecessary. When we take a wrong turn on a road and lose our way, the last thing we need is criticism. It is not helpful to have our driving skills analyzed and evaluated at this point. What we need is a friendly person to give us clear directions" [11].

Ginott warns that "Without compassion and authenticity, techniques fail" [11]. He writes too, "A wise application of parental skills will not ignore individual differences in temperament and personality" [11]. This is as true for a teacher as a parent. And all of the skills and techniques he writes about so well are valid in the Suzuki method, the parent-child-teacher partnership.

In *Peoplemaking,* Virginia Satir writes, "A critical factor in what happens both inside people and between people is the picture of individual worth that each person carries around with him" [33]. Suzuki teachers and parents are trained to build a child's self-esteem.

"To understand the learning problems of another person, particularly a child, we must try to see things as if through their eyes," says John Holt. Speaking of all learning he writes, "Whatever method is used, our experience so far makes it clear that when we use a child's natural desire to explore the new and unknown, and to gain some control over it, without trying to force him faster or further than he feels ready to go, both pupil and teacher have the most fun and the most progress" [17].

Suzuki himself, with his joyous and humourous touch, has the gift of stimulating the child's natural desire to learn. His inspired method points the way for others to enjoy exploring and progressing in the world of music.

LITERATURE CITED

1 Applebaum, Samuel, and Applebaum, Sada, *The Way They Play,* 4 vols, Neptune City, N.J.: Paganiniana Publications, Inc., 1972.

2 Auer, Leopold, *Violin Playing as I Teach It,* New York: Frederick A. Stokes Co., 1921.

3 Bloom, Lois, Hood, Lois, and Lightbrown, Patsy, "Imitation in Language Development," *Cognitive Psychology,* Vol. 6, No. 3, July 1974.

4 Bruner, Jerome S., *Studies in Cognitive Growth,* New York: John Wiley and Sons, Inc., 1966.

5 Carrel, Alexis, *L'Homme cet Inconnue,* trans. Maria Montessori, Paris, 1947.

6 Conway, William, M.D., personal interview, July 6, 1977.

7 Dreikurs, Rudolf, M.D., *Challenge of Parenthood,* New York: Duell, Sloan and Pierce, 1948.

8 Fischer, Bernard, "Suzuki Teaching & Philosophy," *American Music Teacher,* Cincinnati, Ohio: Music Teachers National Association, Vol. XV, No. 5, 1966.

9 Fitts, Paul Morris, and Posner, Michael I., *Human Performance,* Belmont, Calif.: Brooks/Cole Pub. Co., 1967.

10 Galamian, Ivan, *Principles of Violin Playing and Teaching,* Englewood Cliffs, N.J.: Prentice-Hall, 1962.

11 Ginott, Haim, *Between Parent and Teenager,* New York: The MacMillan Co., 1969.

12 Goldberg, Miriam L., *Research on the Talented,* New York: Teachers' College Press, Columbia University, 1965.

13 Grunes, Willa, "A Psychologist Looks at Suzuki Method," *Suzuki Association of the Americas Journal,* Vol. 3, No. 3, Fall 1975.

14 Haley, Jay, *Uncommon Therapy,* New York: Norton, 1973.

15 Havas, Kato, *A New Approach to Violin Playing,* London: Bosworth & Co. Ltd., 1961.
16 Holding, Dennis H., *Principles of Training,* Oxford: Pergamon Press, 1965.
17 Holt, John, *How Children Learn,* New York: Pitman Pub. Corp., 1967.
18 Karel, Leon C., "Enrichment—Why and How," *Perspectives in Music Education,* Bonnie C. Kowall, Ed., Washington, D.C.: Music Educators National Conference, 1966.
19 Keele, Steven W., and Summers, Jeffrey J., "The Structure of Motor Programs," G. E. Stelmach *Motor Control: Issues and Trends,* New York: Academic Press, 1976.
20 Kendall, John D., personal interview, June 23, 1975.
21 Kendall, John D., "The Resurgent String Program in America," *Perspectives in Music Education,* Washington, D.C.: Music Educators National Conference, 1966.
22 *Learning to Read,* Princeton: Educational Testing Service, 1962.
23 Madsen, Clifford, Grier, Douglas, and Madsen, Charles H., Jr., Eds., *Research in Music Behavior,* New York: Teachers College Press, Columbia University, pp. 274–75, 1975.
24 McDonald, Marjorie, M.D., "A Psychoanalyst Looks at Suzuki," *American Suzuki Journal,* Vol. 4, No. 3., Fall 1976.
25 Menuhin, Yehudi, *Violin and Viola,* New York: Schirmer Books, a division of Macmillan Publishing Co., Inc., 1976.
26 Mills, Elizabeth, and Murphy, Sr. Therese Cecile, Eds., *The Suzuki Concept,* Berkeley and San Francisco: Diablo Press, Inc., 1973.
27 Montessori, Maria, *The Absorbent Mind,* Trans. Claude A. Claremont, New York: Holt, Rinehart and Winston, 1967.
28 Piaget, Jean, and Inhelder, Barbel, *The Psychology of*

the Child, Trans. Helen Weaver, New York: Basic Books, Inc., 1969.

29 Pines, Maya, *Revolution in Learning,* New York: Harper & Row, 1967.

30 Polnauer, Fred, and Marks, Morton, *Senso-Motor Study and Its Application to Violin Playing,* Urbana, Ill.: American String Teachers Assn., 1964.

31 *The Republic of Plato,* James Adam, Ed., London: Cambridge University Press, 1909.

32 Sarch, Kenneth, "The Suzuki System: A Critical Evaluation," *American String Teacher,* Mankato, Minn.: The American String Teachers Association, Vol. 20, No. 3, Summer 1970.

33 Satir, Virginia, *Peoplemaking,* Palo Alto, Calif.: Science & Behavior Books, 1972.

34 Seashore, Carl Emil, *The Psychology of Musical Talent,* Boston: Silver, Burdett & Co., 1919.

35 Sheehy, Emma D., *Children Discover Music and Dance,* New York: Teachers College Press, Columbia University, 1968.

36 Shuter, Rosamund, *Psychology of Musical Ability,* London: Methuen & Co., 1968.

37 Starr, William, *The Suzuki Violinist,* Miami, FL: Summy-Birchard Inc., 1967.

38 Suzuki, Shinichi, "The Law of Ability" and "The 'Mother Tongue Method' of Education," excerpts from a talk given to the Japan Institute of Educational Psychology (pamphlet), October 16, 1973.

39 Suzuki, Shinichi, *Nurtured by Love,* Miami, FL: Summy-Birchard Inc., 1969.

40 Tharp, Roland G., and Gallimore, Ronald, "What a Coach Can Teach a Teacher," *Psychology Today,* p. 77, January 1976.

41 Wagner, Michael J., "The Effect of a Practice Report on Practice Time and Musical Performance," *Research in Music Beahvior,* Clifford K. Madsen, Douglas Green, and Charles H. Madsen, Jr., Eds., New York: Teachers College Press, Columbia University, pp. 125–130, 1975.

42 Winn, Edith, *The Child Violinist,* New York: Carl
    Fischer, 1908.
43 Zurcher, William, "The Effect of Model-Supportive
    Practice on Beginning Band Instrumentalists,"
    Research in Music Behaviors, C. Madsen, D. Greer,
    and C. Madsen, Eds., New York: Teachers College
    Press, Columbia University, pp. 131–135, 1975.